DATE DUE		

Out for Trout

by Marie Powell

amicus readers

Mankato, Minnesota

Ideas for Parents and Teachers

Amicus Readers let children practice reading informational texts at the earliest reading levels. Familiar words and concepts with close photo-text matches support early readers.

Before Reading
- Discuss the cover photo with the child. What does it tell him?
- Ask the child to predict what she will learn in the book.

Read the Book
- "Walk" through the book and look at the photos. Let the child ask questions.
- Read the book to the child, or have the child read independently.

After Reading
- Use the word family list at the end of the book to review the text.
- Prompt the child to make connections. Ask: *What other words end with -out?*

Amicus Readers are published by Amicus
P.O. Box 1329, Mankato, MN 56002
www.amicuspublishing.us

Library of Congress Cataloging-in-Publication Data

Powell, Marie, 1958-
  Out for trout / Marie Powell.
    pages cm. -- (Word families)
  ISBN 978-1-60753-514-0 (hardcover) -- ISBN 978-1-60753-545-4 (eBook)
  1. English language--Phonetics--Juvenile literature.
2. English language--Rhyme--Juvenile literature. 3. Vocabulary--Juvenile literature. I. Title.
  PE1135.P66 2013
  428.6--dc23
                        2013006846

Photo Credits: Background Land/Shutterstock Images, cover; Shutterstock Images, 1, 4, 7; Sandra Cunningham/Shutterstock Images, 3; Peter Zachar/ Shutterstock Images, 8, 9, 13; Thinkstock, 11; Marcin Niemiec/Shutterstock Images, 15

Produced for Amicus by The Peterson Publishing Company and Red Line Editorial.

Editor Jenna Gleisner
Designer Marie Tupy
Printed in the United States of America
Mankato, MN
July, 2013
PA 1938
10 9 8 7 6 5 4 3 2 1

Today we are going fishing for **trout**. Dad brings **out** the fishing rods and gear.

4

Dad says it is hard to catch **trout without** bait. We put a worm on the hook.

I **scout** the water for **trout**.

I cast my line and wait.

8

I feel a **trout** tug on my line. Dad helps me pull it in. He says, "Good job, **Sprout**!"

We let my **trout** go. It swims away. I give my sister a turn so she won't **pout**.

My sister catches a **trout**.

We all **shout**, "Hooray!"

I can't wait to tell Mom **about** our fishing trip. I hope we can go **out** for **trout** again soon!

Word Family: -out

Word families are groups of words
that rhyme and are spelled the same.

Here are the -out words in this book:

about
out
pout
scout
shout
sprout
trout
without

Can you spell any other words
with -out?